Little Me
Written by Marka Sawyer
Illustrated by Anna Perez

Illustrations by Anna Perez

Balboa Press books may be ordered through booksellers or by contacting:

Balboa Press
A Division of Hay House
1663 Liberty Drive
Bloomington, IN 47403
www.balboapress.com
1 (877) 407-4847

ISBN: 978-1-5043-3546-1 (sc)
ISBN: 978-1-5043-3547-8 (e)

Library of Congress Control Number: 2015909866

Print information available on the last page.

Balboa Press rev. date: 06/23/2015

Dedicated to

the two that swelled my heart:

Ava and Cady

Call me “Little Me.” I want to tell you who I am and teach you who you are.

Touch your nose with your finger.
You are not your nose.
It is your nose.

You are not your finger.
It is your finger.

Put your hand over your heart. Do you feel the pumping that your heart is doing to get your blood flowing?

You are not your hand;
you are not your heart;
you are not your blood.

You can't see your heart,
but it is there.
You don't know how it
pumps the blood
but it helps keep your
body alive.

Take a deep breath.

Feel your **lungs** filling up

with **air.**

You are not your lungs.

You can run fast with your legs,

but your legs are not who you are.

You are not your body.
It is your body,
but your body is not
who you are.

Little Me is inside you.
Little Me is little you!
And Little Me takes
good care of you.

You know that your fingernails grow and your hair grows.
You know when to eat and when to go to the bathroom.
But you don't think about your nails growing.
You don't tell your hair to grow.

But Little Me does.

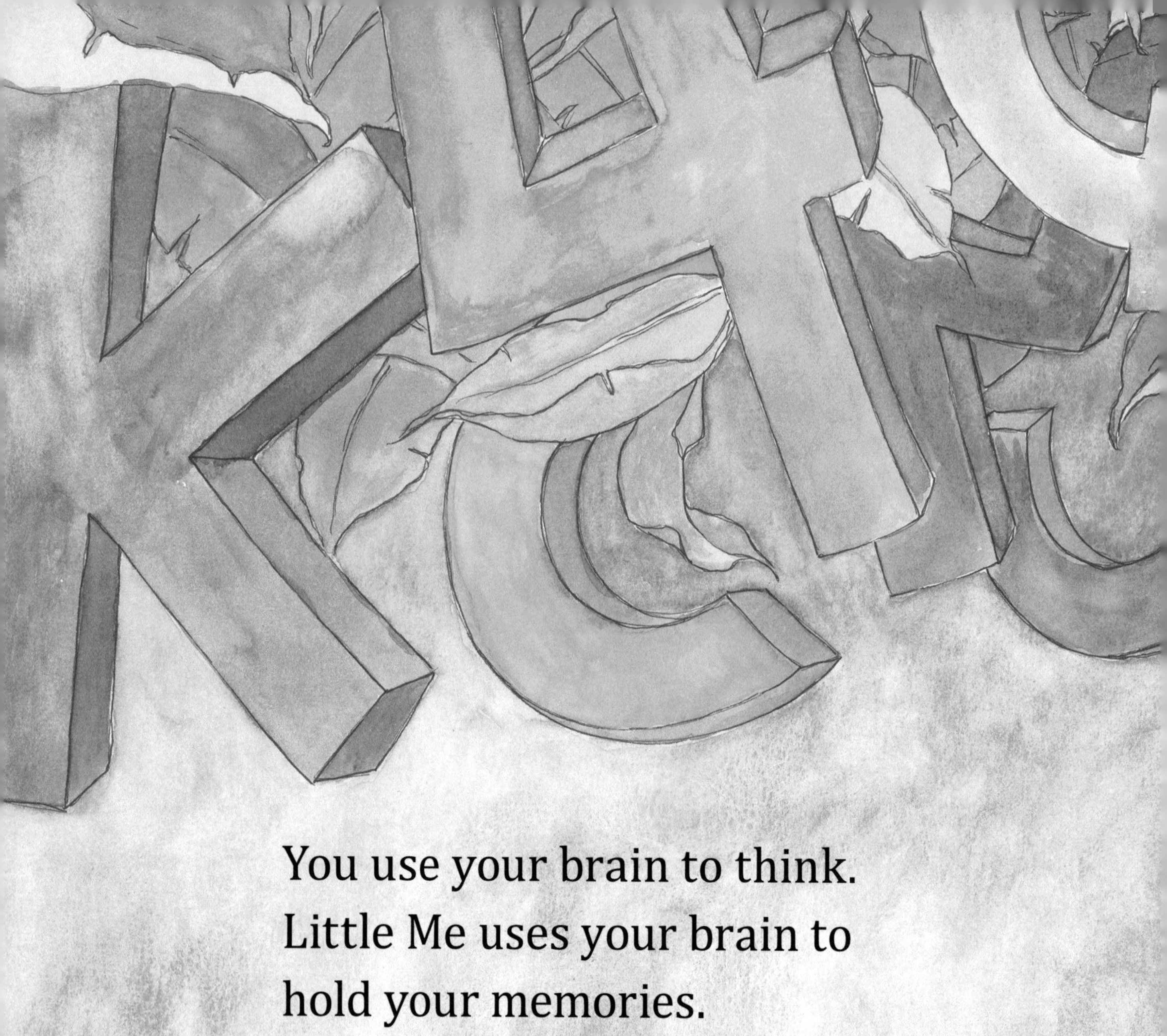

You use your brain to think.
Little Me uses your brain to
hold your memories.
When you learn colors or
numbers, Little Me
remembers them for you.

When you were born, you were 79% water. You need water to grow. When you drink water, Little Me takes it where it needs to go.

Little Me flushes out old stuff and replaces it with new and you keep growing.

Little Me has a lot
of jobs to do.
Little Me will take
care of the insides,
you can take care of
the outside.

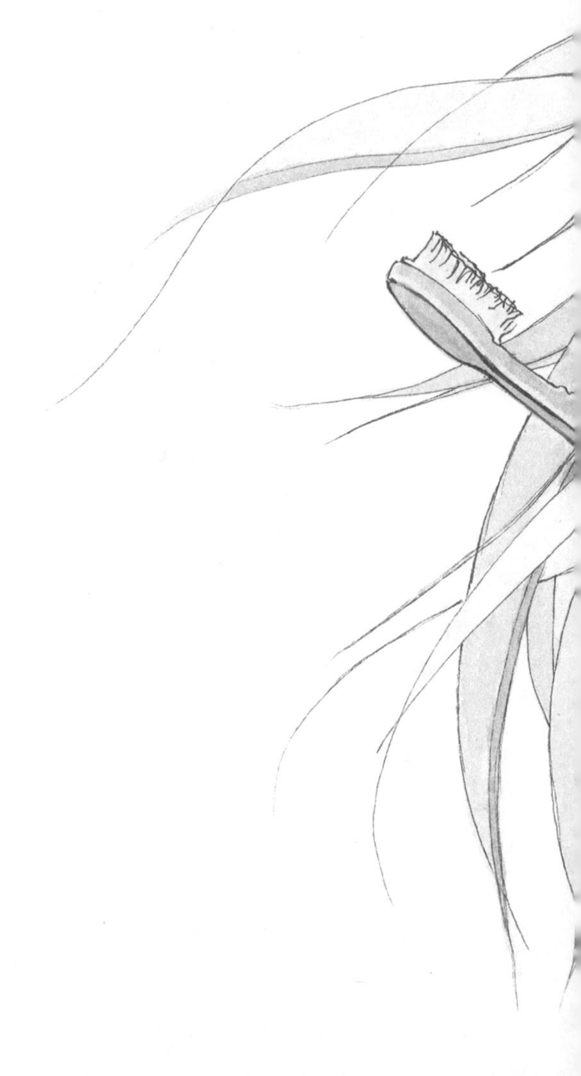

Do you know what
little you has to do;
what you are
responsible for?

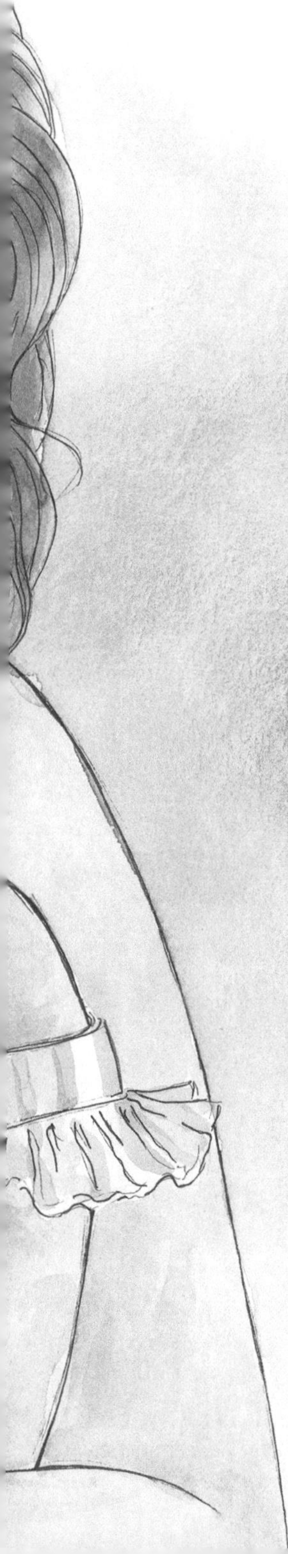

#1
Listen to the people who love you.

#2
Drink lots of water.

#3
BE HAPPY!

Little you can think about
everything you want.
Little Me will listen to your
thoughts and not only
remember them, but will
find a way to make your
thoughts come true.

Nikon
JUKI

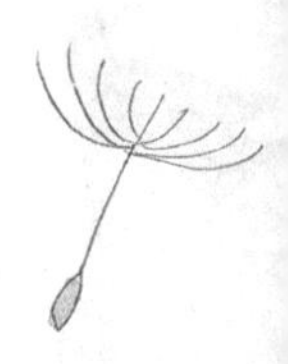

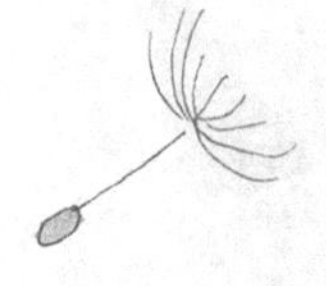

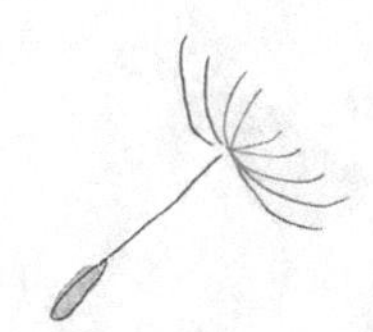

You want to think good
thoughts and be happy.
If you are happy,
everything is good.

So put a smile on your face, our face, and know that Little Me will keep your hair growing and your heart beating.

Little Me will breathe and
will remember your colors
and numbers and the
days of the week
and the months
of the year and
all the things
that will make
you smart.

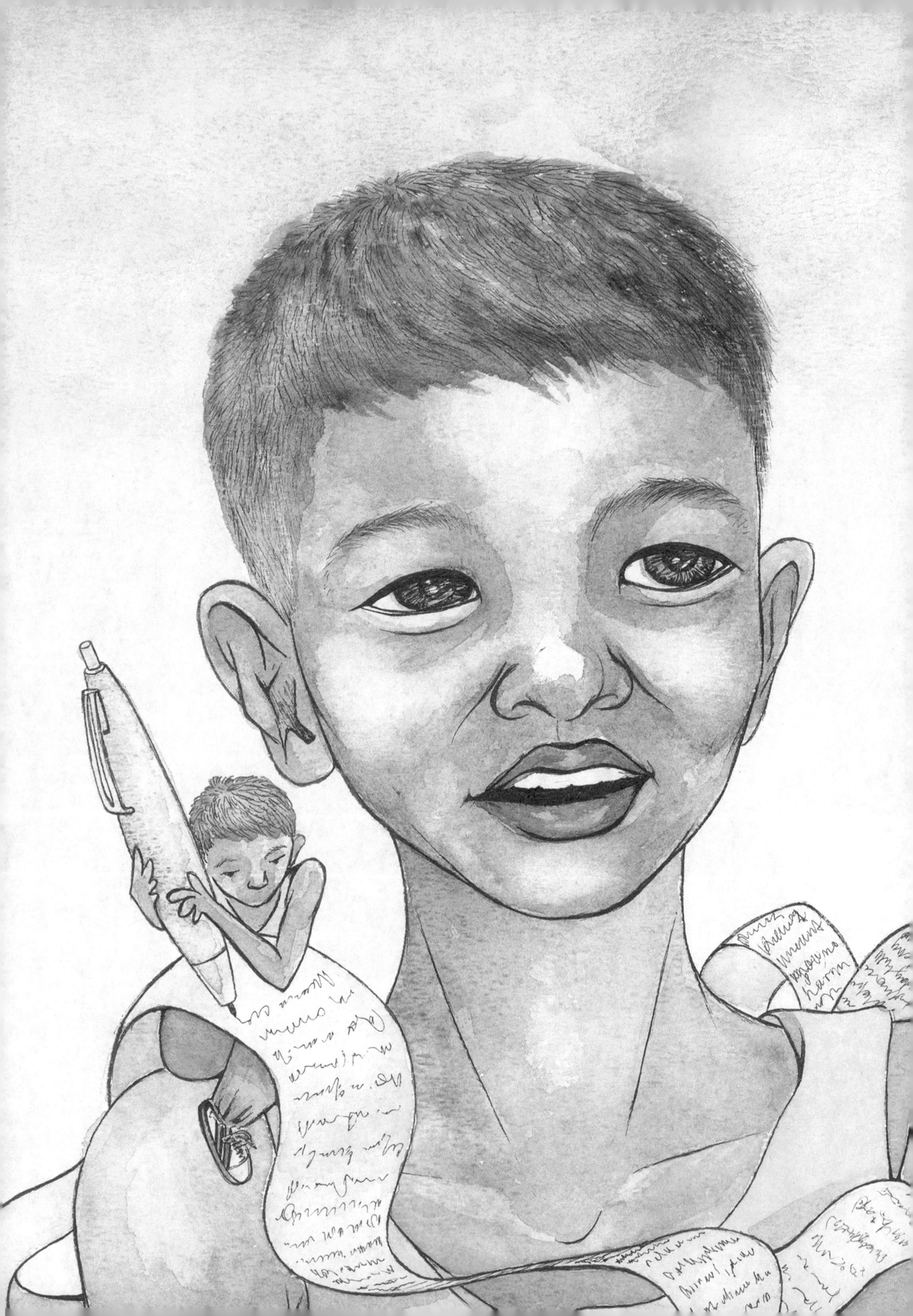

Little Me will remember
everything you think and say.

You are never alone.
You are much more
than what you see in
the mirror.

Little Me is always with you.

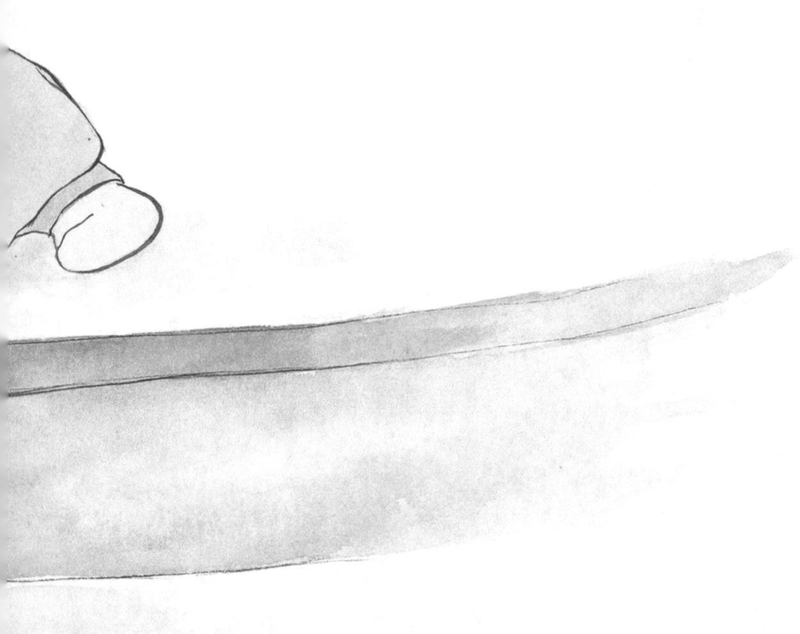

Talk to Little Me about everything.

Little Me does not talk
with words, but you will
learn to listen to Little Me.

Sometimes, just be quiet. And never be afraid to ask Little Me questions. The answers will come. Little Me is very smart and will get you the answers.

The most important thing
is for you to be happy.

Drink lots of water,

take big breaths,

and
BE HAPPY!

Printed in the United States
By Bookmasters